What

was the

Mark of Cain?

By

Samuel Martin

STUDIES IN GENESIS SERIES

Volume One

This volume is dedicated to my wife Sonia. Thank you for your love and for your constant support of my writing efforts.

Recompense to no man evil for evil. Provide things honest in the sight of all men.

If it be possible, as much as lieth in you, live peaceably with all men.

Dearly beloved, avenge not yourselves, but rather give place unto wrath:

for it is written, Vengeance is mine; I will repay, saith the Lord.

Therefore if thine enemy hunger, feed him; if he thirst, give him drink:

for in so doing thou shalt heap coals of fire on his head.

Be not overcome of evil, but overcome evil with good. - Romans 12:17-21

© Copyright 2021 by Samuel Martin

Interior formatting by Dara Stoltzfus

First Edition – Winter 2021

Samuel Martin
Email: info@biblechild.com
Website: www.biblechild.com

ISBN: 978-0-9785339-1-5

The New
Foundation
for
Biblical
Research

Jerusalem

TABLE OF CONTENTS

INTRODUCTION

What was the Mark of Cain?

One of the most puzzling accounts in the book of Genesis concerns the issue of the Mark of Cain. A portion of the account in Genesis 4 shows that the LORD[1] placed a distinguishing "Mark" onto the person of Cain. Scholars for centuries have asked the question: Just what was this "Mark?"

In this new publication, we are going to explore this question with a view to illuminating difficult passages of the Holy Scripture concerning this question. We believe that the LORD has given us all the information that we need within the Scriptures themselves to answer all the questions that we have on most subjects. The question of what the Mark of Cain may have been is no exception. We pray that you find this publication valuable in your Bible study.

Samuel Martin – Jerusalem, Winter 2021

---

[1] Note that throughout this book, we have rendered the holy name of God (Hebrew: יהוה) by the word LORD.

1

Keys to understanding this issue

When first researching this issue, several keys to help understand this question were noted and we will reference them here. They are as follows:

1. It is essential (in the view of the author) to believe that Moses was the author, compiler or first editor of almost all sections of the first five books of the Bible.[2] If a person does not accept this fact, their orientation to the Biblical text may not be one that focuses on looking into other sections of the first five books of the Bible with a view to helping better understand these more mysterious sections in the early chapters of Genesis.

2. It is also important to understand that the early accounts in the book of Genesis have a "Temple symbolism" associated with them. Without this orientation, a person may not be focusing on the themes clearly given in the early sections of Genesis (which are, in the view of the author, completely Temple oriented) and

---

[2] It is noted that Jesus identifies Moses as the author of the first five books of the Bible in Luke 24:44,45

may not be spiritually in tune to these nuances that are essential to understand this narrative about Cain.

3. It is also essential that we be willing to very carefully look at parallel passages throughout Scripture to help us better understand the words that the LORD is using and focus on working with humility and with the best tools that we have available to search the Scriptures to discern God's meaning and intent in regard to the Cain narrative.

4. Lastly, there is a final method that we believe it is important to use. We found it very helpful to focus on an extensive study of the original Hebrew language that makes up the narrative of the life of Cain and what we know about him from Scripture. We noticed when we did this that things began to reveal themselves from the pages of the inspired volume that we had never realized before. By being willing to put all presuppositions up for evaluation and consideration, we found once again that we were able to see things that we never even considered before.

Genesis: A Foundation of Divine Revelation

Dr. E. W. Bullinger, the compiler of the Companion Bible, referred to Genesis saying (I agree with his assessment precisely): "Genesis is the seed-plot of the whole Bible. It is essential to the true understanding of its every part. It is the foundation on which Divine Revelation rests; and on which it is built up. It is not only the foundation of all Truth, but it enters into, and forms part of all subsequent inspiration; ... Genesis is quoted or referred to *sixty* times in the New Testament; and Divine authority is set like a seal on its historical facts."[3]

I could go into all of the connections that Jesus (and the other New Testament writers) has with the Genesis narratives, but these are well known and it is not needed to refer to them here beyond what I have mentioned. It is clear Jesus accepted and taught that all of Genesis was Holy Scripture and I believe He was teaching God's truth. The book of Genesis He had reference to is the same one we have reference to today.

---

[3] E. W. Bullinger, The Companion Bible, Appendix II - See Matt. 19:4-6;24:37-28; Mark 7:4,10;10:3-8; Luke 11:43-51;17:26-29; Jn. 1:51;7:21;8:44-56

2

Summary of the life of Cain
from the Biblical text

To begin this discussion let us first look at the history surrounding Cain and the events mentioned in the Holy Scriptures. The account of his life is found in Genesis 4. It is as follows:

"Now, the man, having come to know Eve his wife, - she conceived and bare Cain, and said, I have gotten a Man, even The LORD! And she went on to bear his brother, Abel, - and Abel became a feeder of sheep, whereas Cain, was a tiller of the ground. So it came to pass, after certain days, (Hebrew: at the end of days meaning the end of the year perhaps) that Cain brought in of the fruit of the ground, a present to the LORD: Abel also even he brought in of the firstlings of his sheep, and of their fat, and the LORD approved of Abel and of his present; but of Cain and his present, he approved not, - and it angered Cain greatly, and his countenance fell. So then the LORD said unto Cain, - Wherefore hath it angered thee, and wherefore hath thy countenance fallen? Shall it not, if thou do right, be lifted up? But if thou do not right, at the entrance a sin-bearer is lying, -

Unto thee, moreover, shall be his longing, though, thou, rule over him. And Cain said unto Abel his brother. Let us go into the field. And it came to pass when they were in the field that Cain rose up against Abel his brother, and slew him. Then said the LORD unto Cain, Where is Abel thy brother? And he said know not, the keeper of my brother, am, I? And he said, What hast thou done? With a voice, the shed-blood[4] of thy brother is crying out to me from the ground, Now therefore, accursed, art thou, - from the ground which hath opened her mouth, to receive the shed-blood of thy brother at thy hand. Though thou till the ground, it shall not go on to give its vigour to thee. A wanderer and a fugitive, shalt thou be in the earth. And Cain said unto the LORD - Greater is my punishment than I can bear. Lo! thou has driven me out, this day, from off the face of the ground And from thy face, shall I be hid, So shall I become a wanderer and a fugitive in the earth. And it shall come to pass, whosoever findeth me, will slay me. And the LORD said to him - Not so, whosoever slayeth Cain seven - fold, shall it be avenged. So the LORD set, for Cain, a sign, that none finding him should smite him. So, Cain went forth from the presence of the LORD, - and dwelt in the Land of Nod, eastward of Eden. And Cain knew his wife, and she conceived, and bare Enoch, - Now it happened that he was building a city, so he called the name of

---

[4] Note that in the original Hebrew, this word דמי is plural; that is, "bloods" and could refer to his blood and that of his descendants. See Genesis Rabbah 22. Thanks to Richard Stodola for drawing my attention to this point.

the city, after the name of his son, Enoch. (Genesis 4:1-17 taken from the J.B. Rotherham Translation – with several minor modifications as indicated within the quotation.)

This is the account of Cain and his life in the early human history in Genesis. What we see from this text is that Cain was the eldest son of Adam and Eve. (v.1) He followed in the footsteps of his father and engaged himself in the pursuit of agriculture. (v.2) We are told that on a certain day[5], that Cain and Abel brought offerings to the LORD. (v.3) We are then told that the LORD accepted Abel's offering, but He did not accept Cain's offering. (v.4-5) Cain was then offered a remedy to this situation by the LORD (v.6-7), but this admonition was rejected by Cain who, then in a thoughtless rage, rose up against his brother Abel and killed him (v.8). The Biblical account of this story of an older brother taking the life of his younger brother appears to take on a particularly horrible aspect when one considers the description by the LORD of the "voice of your brother's blood[6] cries to me from the earth." (v.11) Cain, when questioned about the matter of the

---

[5] Which in Hebrew is the phrase: "at the end of days," which appears to refer to the end of the year and the beginning of the new year, the first of the Hebrew month of Tishri. Note the following quote from my father, Dr. Ernest L. Martin: "First, both men decided to bring offerings at a set time of the year   on a particular day. The phrase "in process of time," in Hebrew, means "at the end of days." It often signified the end of the agricultural (or civil) year (I Kings 17:7) and was near the beginning of Autumn. "Temple Symbolism in Genesis" Foundation for Biblical Research, 1977

[6] This word in Hebrew is plural. See note four.

whereabouts of his brother Abel, lies directly to the LORD, but is convicted when the LORD tells him that his brother's blood on the ground tells a different story. (vs.9-12) When caught in this lie, Cain then admits to the killing and appears to offer a form of acceptance of his sin (v.13). Recognizing that he will be punished by his removal from the presence of the LORD and that of the area of Eden (v.14), Cain points out that due to this situation, it will be hard for him to survive due to individuals seeking him out to take his life (v.14). So, the LORD appoints a "Mark" (Hebrew: אות [ohth]) for Cain to indicate to other people who could come into contact with him, that he is not permitted to be killed and anyone killing Cain will suffer a greater punishment than did Cain himself. (v.15)

This is a general summary of the data we have in the Biblical account associated with Cain and the circumstances that lead up to his receiving the Mark.

3

Some key terms in the narrative of Cain's life, their meaning and significance

We all have preconceptions about Cain and the narrative about his life and these preconceived ideas influence our thinking about Cain and his history. We are all in the same boat on this issue because often times we will simply read a passage over a hundred times or more and still not see something, but then after reading it the 101st time, we may then say: Wait a minute! There is something here that I did not look at before or I am seeing this in a different way. This happened to me many times when studying this issue over the last ten plus years. One of the first places that I noted to be very important in framing this whole issue was the phrase "The Land of Nod."

A new way of looking at the meaning of the phrase "The Land of Nod"

It is hard to imagine how many times we have read over this phrase and thought each time that it had little importance or meaning. In the normal way of looking at this passage, it meant that Cain was to be as the Biblical text said: "a vagabond and a wanderer …"[7] So, Cain in becoming a "vagabond and a wanderer" was then sent to live in the "Land of Nod," which generally we have thought to mean "wandering."

This is the general meaning because the word "wanderer" in Genesis 4:14 and the word "Nod" in Genesis 4:16 are from the same Hebrew root. In fact, the word "Nod" is just a simple transliteration of the Hebrew word. It is just a place generally assigned the meaning "wandering." The word "wanderer" in Hebrew is "*nood.*" Therefore, because of this association between these two words (as well as other usages throughout Scripture of the word "*nood*" and its association with "wandering,") the common definition has become that the Land of Nod refers to a place where Cain (the wanderer) was going to reside (in the Land of Wandering).

This is what we believed until we saw a number of important comparative texts regarding this word that caused us to reconsider this whole issue.

Alternative meanings for the word "nod" in Hebrew

While studying this word and attempting to better understand it, we came to see something very interesting. In Hebrew the phrase "vagabond and wanderer" is in

---

[7] Genesis 4:14 – From the English Translation of Rashi Commentary on Genesis – 1946) Note: King James Version has "fugitive and a vagabond."

Hebrew נע ונד. (noo'ag venood) What we find when we look very closely at these words is that the first word "נע" really has more of an association with the idea of "wandering,"[8] moving,"[9] or being "scattered."[10] It is also true that the word "נד" can also mean "wandering"[11] or being "removed"[12] from one's place.

But it is the fact that the word "nod" in numerous places in Scripture does not necessarily always mean "to move, wander, or being scattered." No, in fact, in the just over 20 places where the Hebrew word "nod" is used, in ten of those cases, the meaning very clearly refers to the idea of "mourning."[13]

Look at one of the key proof texts in this regard. "Now when Job's three friends heard of all this evil that was come upon him, they came … for they had made an appointment together to come to mourn[14] with him and to comfort him."[15] Note also the following: "Weep not for the dead, neither bemoan (Hebrew: tanudu) him, but weep sore for him that goes away:"[16] This text also

---

[8] Amos 4:8; Psalm 59:15(16); II Samuel 15:20; Jeremiah 14:10; Numbers 32:13
[9] Isaiah 6:4; 7:2; 19:1; Proverbs 5:6; II Kings 23:18
[10] Psalm 59:11(12);
[11] Proverbs 26:2
[12] Jeremiah 50:3; 50:8; Psalm 36:11 (12); Isaiah 24:20
[13] See Job 2:11; Psalm 69:20(21); Jeremiah 48:17; Job 42:11; Isaiah 51:19; Jeremiah 15:5; 16:5; 22:10; Nahum 3:7; Jeremiah 31:18
[14] (Hebrew: lanood – which is the infinitive of the verb "nod" and it in this context clearly means "to mourn.")
[15] Job 2:11
[16] Jeremiah 22:10

once again clearly refers to "mourning" by the context and by the use of the word "bemoan."

So what does this mean relative to the use of the phrase "Land of Nod" in Genesis 4:16? It has a great deal to do with it, because perhaps what the intended meaning here is not the "Land of Wandering," but rather the **"Land of Mourning."**

Early Jewish Scholars confirm the idea that "nod" could refer to mourning

If the idea that Cain went into a state of or "Land of Mourning," this little key can provide us with many interesting corollary ideas about him and about what happened to him, especially concerning the Mark of Cain. However, before we refer to some of these, let us note the statements of some early Jewish commentators on this suggestion. Note what the early commentary of Genesis, the Midrash Genesis Rabbah, had to say about this matter:

"Rab said: he made him an example to murderers. Rabbi Hanin said: He made him an example to penitents."[17] What is a "penitent?" Isn't it interesting even in the text of Genesis following the LORD's presentation of the facts to Cain about

---

[17] Midrash Genesis Rabbah 22:12

his brother's blood crying to Him from the ground, when he hears the punishment and realizes that he is going to be banished from the presence of The LORD, look at what Cain says: "My punishment is greater than can be borne."[18]

What we start to see in this section is the idea that Cain expressed remorse and sadness for what he had done to his brother and became the first "penitent" or in simple English: the first **mourner**. He even went into the "Land of Mourning." Now that we have opened this idea up, let us look at some other points concerning this issue.

---

[18] Genesis 4:13

4

Temple Symbolism in Genesis' early chapters

One of the primary keys that we have mentioned in reference to this issue concerns early Temple symbolism in Genesis. We have also referred to the fact that the early sections of Genesis describing Eden and the garden were all written or complied by Moses. These sections have great symbolic teachings to them. These teachings have as their symbolic focus the Holy Temple that was first a tent built by Moses and his contemporaries and later built finally in Jerusalem by Solomon. These early texts in Genesis are full of symbolic teachings if we keep this issue in mind.[19] Let us now review some of these symbolic teachings.

Now, when we start to look at the issues surrounding Temple symbolism in Genesis, it makes good sense to refer to an article written by my late father, Dr. Ernest L. Martin, which brings out these points in a clear way. He noted that: "It was as if God's celestial palace temporarily had come to earth. Even the Garden, the Cherubim of the Garden, the altar built by Cain and Abel, the Land of Eden,

---

[19] For more information, please see the paper "Temple Symbolism in Genesis" by Ernest L. Martin, FBR 1977

and the Land of Nod are all connected with the temple symbolism and are direct images of God's heavenly abode."[20]

The first point we wish to discuss concerns the issue of the language used to describe the various times when the LORD and Adam and Eve had contact. Note the following: "In the Garden our first parents were able to talk face to face with the LORD. But note an important point. They only had conversations with Him at certain times of the day. They did not see Him on all occasions. It was "in the cool of the day" that they came into "the presence of the LORD" (Gen. 3:8). The expressions "cool of the day" and "the presence of the LORD" were a part of the language associated with the Temple. "The cool of the day" was the period when the sun got lower in the sky and the cool sea breezes normally swept over Israel. This was the time of the evening sacrifice (I Kings 18:36; Daniel 9:21) about three in the afternoon. ... At these times the people were then reckoned as being "in the presence of God" (II Chronicles 20:19)."[21]

Note also that the incident where the heavenly beings, the Cherubim, are mentioned in the early section of Genesis and how this relates to Temple symbolism. "So he drove out the man; and he placed at the east of the garden of Eden Cherubim, and a flaming sword which turned every way, to keep the way of the tree of life" (Genesis 3:22-24). This episode has some very significant

---

[20]Ernest Martin, Temple Symbolism in Genesis: Foundation for Biblical Research: 1977
[21] *ibid.*

features associated with it. Observe that they were expelled east of the Garden. Cherubim (angelic beings - later connected with temple symbolism) were also stationed at the east gate to the Garden with a flaming sword to prevent Adam and Eve from re-entering.[22] The Cherubim guarded the east entrance (the only gate) into the Garden and forbade anyone to enter. We will see in a moment that these features represent precise arrangements found in the later tabernacle and temple."[23]

The Genesis narrative relates to the Garden of Eden and is full of Temple Symbolism

When we look at the whole narrative of Genesis, we find the following parallels which are given in Genesis and relate to other sections of the Bible related to the Temple. Let us just give a short summary here.[24]

---

[22] A question we have to ask here concerns the issue of whether these cherubim ever permitted Adam back into the Garden? Based upon Temple Symbolism, we might find that they just might have allowed it at a specific time.

[23] *ibid.*

[24] For a more detailed examination of these points, see: Dr. Ernest Martin, Temple Symbolism in Genesis: Foundation for Biblical Research: 1977 and the book Secrets of Golgotha (Second Edition: ASK Publications, 1996) which has several sections which discuss these points.

Temple Type in Genesis	Temple Anti-Type
1. The Inner Garden[25]	The Holy of Holies[26]
2. The Larger Garden[27]	The Holy Place[28]
3. Cain and Abel's Altar[29]	The Altar of Burnt Offering[30]
4. Eden[31]	The Camp of Israel[32]

---

[25] "The Book of Jubilees stated that the inner "Garden" was analogous to the sanctuary in the Temple (Jubilees 8:19 and compare Jub. 3:10-12)." (Martin, Secrets of Golgotha: ASK Pubs: 1996, p. 238); See also Gen. 3:3 talking about the "midst of the garden."

[26] "The Holy Place of the Temple into which only the priests could enter to perform their administrations was acknowledged as "the Garden" section of the Land of Eden. This was where Adam and Eve lived at first before they sinned. Further inside "the Garden" was an inner part to which God would appear at specified times. This was like the Holy of Holies." (*ibid.*); See also Exodus 26:33 & Numbers 7:89.

[27] "These matters [noted in footnotes 17 & 18] are good evidence to show that this "Garden" area was represented by the Holy Place in the Temple of Solomon." (*ibid.*)

[28] "The Bible records that Solomon "carved all the walls of the house [the Holy Place] round about with carved figures of cherubim and palm trees and open flowers within and without" [that is, the carvings were on the inside walls of the Holy Place as well as on its outside walls] (I Kings 6:29; see also Ezekiel 41:18 where the prophet also decorated his future, prophetic Temple in the same way)." (*ibid.*)

[29] "It was only in the "Garden" section of Eden that they could no longer enter. And then, sometime later their two sons Cain and Abel built an altar. This was positioned before the entrance to "the Garden" (in which God was supposed to dwell)." (*ibid.* pgs.238-239); See also Genesis 4:4,5.

[30] "Concerning the sacred furniture in the Tabernacle and Temple this altar was analogous to the Altar of Burnt Offering which was positioned just east of the entrance to the Holy Place [or "the Garden"]." (*ibid.* pg. 239)

[31] Genesis 2,3 & 4

[32] Deuteronomy 23:11,13,14

Temple Type in Genesis	Temple Anti-Type
5. The Land of Nod[33]	Outside the Camp of Israel[34]
6. The Altar for Cain[35]	The Miphkad Altar[36]
7. City of Cain[37]	Cities of Refuge[38]

---

[33] "What does this mean relative to the use of the phrase "Land of Nod" in Genesis 4:16? It has a great deal to do with it, because perhaps what the intended meaning here is not the "Land of Wandering," but rather the **"Land of Mourning."**

[34] Numbers 2 and Hebrews 13:13

[35] "While east of Eden and in the Land of Nod, God promised Cain a sacrifice for sin if he ever did wrong. God said to Cain: "if you do not well, sin [a sin offering] couches at the door" (Gen.4:7). The couching of this sin offering for Cain meant (in the usage of the word in other contexts of the Bible) that it would be so weighted down with "sin" that it would have to couch at the door because of the heavy weight. Before what door was this sin offering placed? Since all sin offerings had to be presented "in the presence" of God for acceptance (and since God dwelt in inner sanctum of "the Garden" in the Land of Eden), Cain's sin offering was prophesied to couch before the door represented the eastern gate to the Land of Eden." (*ibid.* pg. 239)

[36] "In the Tabernacle and Temple this altar on which Cain's sin offering would be placed by the Miphkad Altar located on the Mount Olives and outside the Temple (even outside the camp of Ezekiel 43:21)." (*ibid.* pg. 239)

[37] Genesis 4:17 – This text is shown to refer later to the cities that Moses founded as cities of refuge. See below.

[38] "Indeed, we find also, that the Eastern quarter [that is, in this case, the Land of Nod] always forms a place of refuge for murderers, as it is said: (Deut: 4:41) "Then Moses set aside 3 cities of refuge towards the place of sun-rise." Rosenbaum & Silbermann, "Rashi's Commentary on the Pentateuch," p.19. Shapiro/Valentine & Co., London, 1946.

Early Jewish scholars agree with this idea of the early chapters of Genesis being symbolic of the Temple

How have Jewish scholars looked at this issue of comparing the narratives we find in Genesis to those associated with the later Temple of God? We find much evidence of their belief in the validity of such comparisons. Note the following:

"Indeed, we find also, that the Eastern quarter [that is, in this case, the Land of Nod] always forms a place of refuge for murderers, as it is said: (Deuteronomy 4:41) "Then Moses set aside three cities of refuge towards the place of sun-rise."[39]

This text helps us put the Mosaic narrative in its proper Temple oriented context.

Now, in orienting ourselves to this Temple type/anti-type, we can now start to better put the flesh on the skeleton of what the Mark of Cain really may have been.

---

[39] Rosenbaum & Silbermann, "Rashi's Commentary on the Pentateuch," p.19. Shapiro & Valentine and Co., London, 1946.

5

Cain's age when he killed Abel and its relevance

We are not told precisely in the book of Genesis when this event happened, but may we make speculations in this regard? We are told that Cain and Abel were the first children of Adam and Eve (Genesis 4:1,2). The births of these two children preceded the birth of Seth who was born in the 130th year of Adam's life (Genesis 5:3). This same Seth, the Scripture teaches, produced his first child. Enoch, at the age of 105 (*ibid.*, 5:6) We are not told precisely, but could it be that Cain and Abel were born sometime just after Adam passed his 100th year? We are not told when Cain was born, but if Cain was born when, for example, Adam was, say 105 years old, then Abel for the sake of this example, was born at least a year or perhaps two or even three years later.[40] You would have Cain becoming 12 in Adam's 117th year and his brother, Abel, becoming 11 or 10 (or perhaps 9) in Adam's 118th or 119th years (or 120th year if there was a three year gap between the children).[41]

---

[40] Adam and Eve probably had about an equal number of female children, which must also be considered here.

[41] Note: We have to have Cain and Abel at least reaching to these ages when we consider the information in the texts about their taking on the responsibilities of work in tending a field and in taking care of flocks. Children smaller than these ages could not, under normal circumstances, take on these duties.

One of the interesting things about this issue concerning the ages of Cain and Abel is that we have a source that seems to indicate this. In the Midrash Rabbah it quotes Lamech, a descendant of Cain, who says the following: "Did 'I' slay Abel who was a man in height, **but a child in years,** that my descendants should be exterminated on account of this sin (the sin of Cain who killed Abel)."[42] It is interesting that we do find some evidence that seems to point to the youthfulness of Abel (and also by extension of Cain himself).

Since we do not have a clear statement in the Bible about the number of years between these children, we have to look to other sections of the Bible that might help us to better understand this issue. One thing that can help us perhaps is to look at other figures in the Bible, particularly in these earlier sections and look at families and see if we have any clues about the normal spacing of children in these earlier periods.

Much of the data is very terse and short, but if we will pay close attention to the information that we do have, we might just find some clues to help us better understand what was happening here in this early section of Genesis.

Since Moses was the writer of this section,[43] perhaps it makes good sense to look at his life. We are told in the Bible that Moses had a brother named Aaron

---

[42] Bereshit Rabbah 23 in Rosenbaum & Silbermann, "Rashi's Commentary on the Pentateuch," p.21. Shapiro & Valentine & Co. London, 1946.

[43] See Luke 24:44,45

and that his brother was three years older than he was.[44] In addition, a careful study of the life of Moses' older sister Miriam will show that she was born at least six years before Moses was.[45] We find some evidence in the Bible, which indicates that there may have been a tendency among the ancient Hebrews to space their children about three years apart. This is because of the ancient custom of weaning children from the breast finally at age three.[46] We find this indicated in other sections of the Bible as well where the tendency to wait until one child was weaned before seeking to get pregnant again is referenced. Note what is spoken of the wife of the prophet Hosea:

"Now when she had weaned Lo-ruhamah, she conceived, and bore a son."[47]

The idea of weaning as the chosen method to "complete" or "ripen" a child is something that is found in the Hebrew verb (*gah-mal*) that the word "to wean" comes from. Strong's Hebrew Concordance defines this word as "A primitive root; to *treat* a person (well or ill), that is, *benefit* or *requite*; by implication (of *toil*)

---

[44] Exodus 7:7

[45] See Bullinger's Companion Bible Appendix 50, Chronology Charts.

[46] Mc'lintock & Strongs: Cyclopedia of Biblical, Theological & Ecclesiastical Literature, vol. II, pg. 243, article. '*child*,' which refers to Genesis 21:8; Exodus 2:7,9; I Samuel 1:22-24; II Chronicles 31:16 and Matthew 21:16

[47] Hosea 1:8

to *ripen*, that is, (specifically) to *wean*: - bestow on, deal bountifully, do (good), recompense, requite, reward, ripen, serve, wean, yield." There is a strong tendency to believe that in the Biblical period, God initially passed down the idea to Adam and Eve that once you had a baby, it was preferred to "ripen" that child through breast feeding for just over two years and then a family could think about adding another child after the previous one had been "ripened."

Now, since we are not told, can we, with the information we do have, make some reasonable speculations regarding the age of Cain when he committed this killing? Naturally, Cain must have been at least one year older (probably three years is more likely) than his younger brother Abel, but we are not told precisely how old they were when the killing took place. Can we, however, make some educated guesses from the Biblical text? Perhaps.

It is interesting that in the time of Moses that the death penalty applied to numerous situations. For example, there was a man who suffered the effects of capital punishment for gathering sticks on the Sabbath. (Numbers 15:32) This individual, who died in the book of Numbers, is called a "man" (Hebrew: *ish*). In light of this issue, it is seemingly very uncharacteristic (under the circumstances where Cain did kill Abel) of the LORD that the death penalty was not assigned to Cain. How was it that this man who committed the crime of working on the Sabbath suffered the death penalty, but Cain who took a life, did not? Why was

27

this? His offense seemingly was greater than that of the man who lost his life for picking up sticks on the Sabbath? After all, he did kill his brother.

We also have the story of Uzzah at the ark. Uzzah lost his life for reaching out to steady the ark in violation of the Law,[48] but once again Cain took a life and received a punishment that does not seem congruent with the crime? Or did he?

We have another story in the Bible in this regard. Scripture tells us that the LORD brought a retribution of capital punishment on Onan due to the fact that he failed to perform the legal obligation to continue the name of his departed brother.[49] Onan, due to his ability to perform this act of "raising up seed to his brother," was clearly physically able to perform this task (and there is every indication from the text that he understood the legal obligation), but failed to do so, thereby coming under the divine retribution. Now, let us look practically at how this matter relates to the issue of Cain and the taking of Abel's life.

Is it possible though that Cain did not commit a premeditated murder, but rather in an episode of youthful rage, his anger got the best of him and he killed his brother? As sad as this story is, we in the modern world hear horrible stories of young people who, for one or a hundred reasons, kill one another, but malice aforethought is absent. These cases today are called "manslaughter." We

---

[48] II Sam. 6:3 CBTEL vol. X, p. 689 says Uzzah's sin was he wasn't an Aaronic priest and ineligible to touch the ark.
[49] Genesis 38:11

in the modern world are even familiar with terms related to degrees of manslaughter, which are found in courtroom parlance.[50] Manslaughter is a very different thing than premeditated murder. Could it be that Cain's sin, while a death did indeed take place, was looked on differently by the LORD?

One thing that is for certain is the fact that Abel was at least about a year younger than Cain. In this regard, we ask is it possible that both of them were under the age of 13? The age of 13 is the time in the life of a young Jewish male when that "boy" begins the process to becoming a "man" and then he is obligated to begin keeping all of the commandments (Hebrew: *mitzvot*) of God.[51] Could it be that what we are reading here is an incident involving what we today would call "teenagers? Perhaps the reason the LORD did not demand the death penalty of Cain was that he had not yet reached the age of accountability, or, was this a case of negligent homicide or manslaughter? We cannot say 100% for sure, but we can say this: Cain killed his brother.

Regarding the age of Cain, the Bible does make one fact clear. All of the events associated with Cain and Abel took place prior to the time that Cain

---

[50] http://www.law.ua.edu/colquitt/crimmain/crimmisc/jurymur.htm – This link points to two degrees of murder and two degrees of manslaughter.
[51] For information on 13 being the age of accountability, see Encyc. Judaica, "Bar Mitzvah" v. 4, p.243.)

married and had his own children. Of this we can be certain because of the indications mentioned directly in the Biblical text.[52]

Other keys that shows that Cain was not recognized as a murderer by the LORD

Another little key that we have referenced earlier in this volume is that the city that Cain built was seen by early Jewish scholars to be analogous to the cities of refuge set up by Moses.[53] However, isn't it interesting that we note that these cities served the purpose to be locations where a "manslayer" could flee when he killed a person inadvertently?

"Then you shall appoint you cities to be cities of refuge for you; that the slayer may flee there, which kills any person at unawares."[54]

The following text relates the same idea:

---

[52] Genesis 4:17
[53] Rosenbaum & Silbermann, "Rashi's Commentary on the Pentateuch," p.19. Shapiro & Valentine and Co., London, 1946. In addition, see all of Numbers 35
[54] Numbers 35:11

"These six cities shall be a refuge, both for the children of Israel, and for the stranger, and for the sojourner among them: that every one that kills any person unawares may flee there."[55]

Another vital point in the Genesis narrative about Cain and his leaving to go to the Land of Nod and build of a city there, it is interesting to note that by the use of the word "blood," which as we have pointed out earlier is in the plural, this seems to point to the future idea of the "avenger of blood."[56] While this may be the case, the important point to remember in this context, is that the LORD made it very clear that Cain's crime, while heinous, did not merit the death penalty. He also made it clear that anyone who took it upon himself to avenge Abel's death would suffer a worse punishment.

"And the LORD said unto him, Verily, Who so ever slays Cain, it shall be avenged sevenfold."[57]

It seems through this statement that we see that Cain's act was one, which did not fall within the later idea of a "life for life",[58] and that law did not apply here

---

[55] Numbers 35:15
[56] See Deuteronomy 19:16; 19:12 and Joshua 20:3,5 & 9.
[57] Genesis 4:15
[58] Exodus 21:23,24)

because of mitigating circumstances. One thing though is clear, Cain did kill his brother and he did not suffer capital punishment. Something else took place that did not involve the death penalty. Believe it or not, in this event, we can start to see what might have been the Mark of Cain.

6

Scholarly and Rabbinical theories
on Cain's Mark

Scholars have offered numerous opinions as to what this "Mark" was. Early Jews offered several ideas as to the identification of this "Mark." Some looked on the sign as something totally external from Cain. "God gave him a dog for protection … "[59] Others felt it was some type of a disease. "He [the LORD] caused leprosy to break out on him, as you read, 'And it shall come to pass, if they will not believe thee, neither hearken to the voice of the first sign [Exodus 4:8 – This word sign (Hebrew: *oth*) in this verse is the same word used to describe the "Mark" given to Cain]"[60] We also have the following: "Abba Jose said: 'He made a horn grow out of him."[61]

Others have suggested other possible solutions. Wenham says some commentators' call this sign a "tattoo."[62] He also notes Boer felt "the sign for Cain is simply his name, which sounds like the Hebrew word *yuqqam*, meaning "shall be punished."[63]

---

[59] Midrash Genesis Rabbah, 22:12)
[60] *ibid.*
[61] *ibid.*
[62] *Word Biblical Commentary* - Genesis (Ch. 1-15), p. 109
[63] *ibid.*

We see from these examples that this is an issue that people have discussed and many possible suggestions have been brought forward as to what was the "Mark" of Cain. Many of these ideas are certainly compelling, but we are going to have to continue our search to find out what the real "Mark" of Cain may have been.

7

Cain's Separation and the Clue to the Mark

When we first realize that Cain was placed in the "Land of Mourning," it is important to point out that he was now placed in a location and was given a designation of being in a perpetual state of mourning. Cain was now physically "separated" from the LORD. When we look at the Temple symbolism and the geographical separation mentioned in Genesis, we see that Cain was now not only outside the location where the LORD lived in the Garden, but he was taken outside of the whole Garden and even outside the whole of the Land of Eden. The closest that Cain could get to the place where the LORD symbolically lived was the entrance to Eden. Therefore, he was, unlike Adam and Eve, who continued to be allowed to live within Eden, not allowed to remain in that closer position to God. He was for all practical purposes "separated" from the LORD.

Now considering that Cain was now "separated" from God's presence and if all of this narrative in this early section of Genesis is full of Temple symbolism (which it is), do we start to have some clues as to what the Mark of Cain might have been? The answer is yes. Cain was given the outward sign of mourning which was well known in the Jewish faith: he became a lifetime Nazarite, or a "separated one," which is what the Hebrew word means.

The Nazarite Vow – What it means

When first researching this issue, I knew about the Nazarites and what their vows entailed. Dr. Ernest L. Martin summarized this issue as follows:

"While it can easily be shown that ordinary Jewish men wore their hair short, did not a special group known as Nazarites among the Jews let their hair grow without cutting it? Only when Jewish men were under a Nazarite vow which normally lasted for 30 days and rarely beyond 100 days (see M'Clintock and Strong, Cyclopedia, vol. VI.pp.881,882) or when in short periods of mourning (see early Jewish commentaries on Leviticus 10:6) did Jewish men refrain from going to the barber. And interestingly, during the time Jewish men would let their hair grow (not to long lengths like the hair of women), they were forbidden by God to enter his Temple. The Hebrew word from which the term Nazarite gets its origin means "separation." While there are men under a Nazarite vow who have devoted themselves to contrition and humility (even shame for some of their actions), they were required to stay out of God's Temple during their period of vow (that is, they were to stay away from God's own home.)"[64]

---

[64]Ernest L. Martin, Secrets of Golgotha (second edition) pgs. 348-349, ASK Publications, 1996.

This is an exceedingly important quote and it speaks about the exact circumstances that came upon Cain. Cain was:

1. Separated from God and given the designation "mourner"

2. Not allowed to enter God's presence

3. In a state of punishment for his sins

4. Placed into the Land of Mourning

5. Living in a region that symbolically came to be associated with mourners, penitents and those who were in a state of perpetual contrition, shame and humility for their actions

6. Given a distinguishing "Mark" to his appearance that could be visible to others

It is important to refer also to the commentaries mentioned in the previous quote from Leviticus 10:6. Note the following from Rashi's Commentary on the Pentateuch:

"(6) [ראשיכם אל תפרעו] means, let not your hair grow long (cf. Num. VI:5) (Siphra). From this (from the fact that Scripture forbade these particular mourners to let their hair grow long) it follows that an אבל (one mourning the death of a near relative) is forbidden to cut his hair. Moses' words therefore signified: Ordinarily an אבל may not cut his hair, but ye, disturb ye not the joy of the Omnipresent God by displaying signs of mourning. (M. Katan 14b.)[65]

When we take this evidence given in this quote, as plainly as the writer could indicate it, those in mourning (which Cain certainly was) did not cut their hair. This evidence fits well with the suggestion we are making here.

When we look at all the evidence, we can see that the best logical and symbolically accurate designation would be to say that Cain was given the outward appearance of a lifetime Nazarite and that the Mark of Cain represents long hair.

---

[65] Rosenbaum & Silbermann, "Rashi's Commentary on the Pentateuch," Vol. II, pg.39. Shapiro & Valentine & Co., London, 1946.

Other books by Samuel Martin

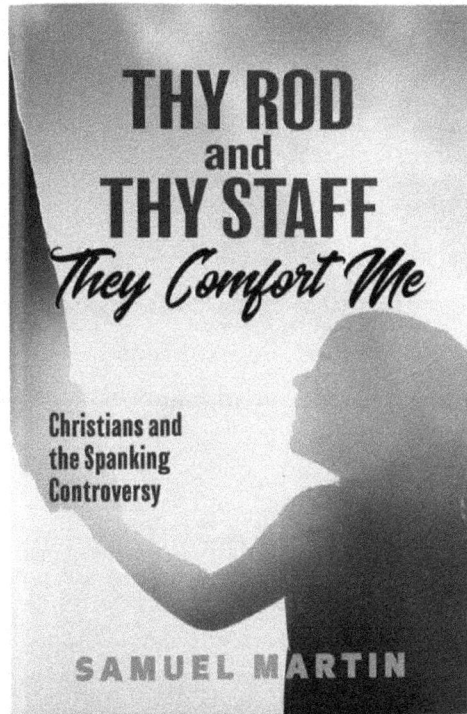

Thy Rod and Thy Staff, They Comfort Me: Christians and the Spanking Controversy – Available free here in soft copy – www.biblechild.com or on Amazon in hard copy – https://www.amazon.com/gp/product/0978533909/ref=dbs_a_def_rwt_bibl_vppi_i1

Reviews of the book

Thy Rod and Thy Staff, They Comfort Me:

Christians and the Spanking Controversy

"I've had a chance to read through your manuscript and I find it very interesting! I think you've made an important contribution, especially to contextualizing biblical ideas about childrearing. I hope you will find a publisher for this book. I'm sure many others would benefit from learning of your research."

Dr. Dawn Devries, John Newton Thomas Professor of Systematic Theology, Union Theological Seminary, USA and contributor to the ground breaking volume "The Child in Christian Thought" (Eerdmans: 2000)

"This is not an easy read, but it is one any Christian who desires to be true to the Bible in the first instance should take time to read. ... In my view this study is a definitive reading of the biblical texts for Christians and non-Christians alike."

Rev. Alistair McBride, Scots Presbyterian Church – Hamilton, New Zealand (see www.repeal59.blogspot.com - July 25 2006)

"Many thanks for sending me a copy of your book. Since I, like so many, cannot read Hebrew, I found your analysis of language fascinating and persuasive. Your exploration of these complex issues is thorough and convincing"

Dr. Philip Greven, Professor Emeritus, Rutgers University, author of "Spare the Child: The Religious Roots of Punishment and the Psychological Impact of Physical Abuse" (Random House, 1992)

"These and other verses, as well as the overall teaching about disciplining children in the Bible is ably discussed by Jerusalem-based Christian biblical scholar Samuel Martin, who has produced a wonderful book, Thy Rod and Thy Staff They Comfort Me: Christians and the Spanking Controversy, available as a free PDF download here with no cost or obligation. Martin has been joined by a significant number of other informed Christian scholars and commentators who are questioning the both the traditional translation and interpretation of these overly quoted verses from the book of Proverbs. I recommend Martin's work for those biblically oriented folk out there who have wondered about what the Bible really says regarding using corporeal punishment of any kind to discipline children—or for that matter anyone who wants to be more informed on this controversial topic."

Professor James D. Tabor, Chair (2004-2014) of the Department of Religious Studies at the University of North Carolina, where he has taught since 1989. He is currently Professor of ancient Judaism and early Christianity.

"I want to take my hat off to Samuel Martin and say, Thanks!

When I think about Samuel Martin, what comes to mind is a contemporary and contextualized, this-world version of William Wilberforce. He certainly has Wilberforce blood running through his veins. He is a Christian living in Jerusalem with an interest in connecting to the rest of the world in ways that are helpful and strategic about how to live out ones faith. Check his website: samuelmartin.blogspot.com. You will find interesting discussions about various biblical subjects.

In addition to being a blogger, Samuel is an author. I just finished reading his book Thy Rod and Thy Staff They Comfort Me: Christians and the Spanking Controversy. I ordered the book from a California source and had it delivered to a Canadian residence http://www.archivescalifornia.com/. Unlike more academic books that I tend to write, which can often be inaccessible to average readers (!), Samuel Martin does a

41

good job of writing with an easy-to-understand touch. For me the greatest benefit in reading his book was to see how a movement towards an anti-spanking position can be developed through Jewish sources and readings of Scripture (as well as Christian ones). He comes to similar conclusions that I do regarding the spanking controversy but his path through the biblical material is quite different - a fascinating read.

Blogger, author and, most importantly, activist! My third thanks to Samuel is that he has reminded me of my own need to be at least to some extent . . . an activist. He has not done this by way of harassment. No, he has shown me this through his own life and example. He would be happy to know that recently I have broken out of my insulated scholarly circles and actually done a handful of radio interviews. Now that is a stretch for a stuffy, old professor of New Testament. Through his own activist work quite extensive as I have watched from afar he is changing the world one person at a time. He does so often by putting people together in ways that help to bring influence on those who perhaps would otherwise not listen. Samuel has reminded me of something that is easily forgotten in the ivory towers of academia, namely, that ideas only work to the degree that there are people willing to influence (other) people about those ideas. So, on three accounts my hat is off to Samuel Martin - blogger, author and activist." - Professor William Webb

Dr. Bill Webb is Adjunct Professor of Biblical Studies at Tyndale Seminary. He has worked as a pastor, chaplain, and professor over a span of over twenty years. In addition to conference speaking ministry, he has published several articles and books, including Returning Home (Sheffield Press, 1993), Slaves, Women, and Homosexuals (IVP, 2001), Discovering Biblical Equality (two chapters; IVP, 2005), Four Views on Moving from the Bible to Theology (one view and responses; Zondervan, 2009), Corporal Punishment in the Bible: A Redemptive Hermeneutic for Troubling Texts (IVP, 2011).

Other books by Samuel Martin

THY ROD and THY STAFF
They Comfort Me BOOK II

14 years in the making, Samuel Martin returns with his second volume in the series, "Thy Rod and Thy Staff, They Comfort Me," further strenthening an already compelling case against corporal punishment in this new book, focused on the New Testament book of Hebrews chapter 12:5-11, which is a key text quoted by many Christians today in their belief in corporal punishment.

FEATURES OF THIS NEW BOOK ARE:
- The original manuscript order of Hebrews and its importance?
- Who wrote Hebrews and why that is important?
- If Paul wrote Hebrews, why did he not identify himself openly?
- What geographical region was Hebrews written to?
- When was the book of Hebrews written?
- What is the main subject of the book of Hebrews?
- Who is the book of Hebrews relevant for today?
- How does this survey of Hebrews link to our understanding of the debate concerning spanking children in the 21st century?

The first book in the series, 'Thy Rod and Thy Staff, They Comfort Me: Christians and the Spanking Controversy,' (published in 2006) was not sold, but has been available as a free download on numerous sites on the web and through www.biblechild.com. A printed version is now also available for purchase through Amazon.

THY ROD and THY STAFF *They Comfort Me* BOOK II

SAMUEL MARTIN

THY ROD and THY STAFF
They Comfort Me
BOOK II

The Book of Hebrews and the Corporal Punishment of Children in the Christian Context

SAMUEL MARTIN

Thy Rod and Thy Staff, They Comfort Me: Book II – The Book of Hebrews and the Corporal Punishment of Children in the Christian Context – Available on Amazon in hard copy.

https://www.amazon.com/Samuel-Martin/e/B00HP94ZZA/ref=dp_byline_cont_pop_book_1

Reviews of the book

Thy Rod and Thy Staff, They Comfort Me: Book II

The Book of Hebrews and the Corporal

Punishment of Children in the Christian Context

"Samuel Martin does a good job of writing with an easy to understand touch ... He comes to similar conclusions that I do regarding the spanking controversy."

- Professor William Webb, Adjunct Professor of Biblical Studies, Tyndale Seminary, Canada and author of the book "Corporal Punishment in the Bible: A Redemptive Movement Hermeneutic for Troubling Texts" (InterVarsity, 2011)

"I think you present a well-crafted argument."

Pastor Crystal Lutton, author of "Biblical Parenting"

"a very provocative and stimulating perspective of Hebrews."

Clay Clarkson, author of "Heartfelt Discipline: Following God's Path of Life to the Heart of Your Child."

Other books by Samuel Martin

Available on Amazon:

https://www.amazon.com/gp/product/0978533933/ref=dbs_a_de f_rwt_bibl_vppi_i0

Reviews of the book

Thy Rod and Thy Staff, They Comfort Me: Book III

A Biblical Study on Maternal Intuition and its link

to the Issue of Spanking Children

From the Amazon page:

https://www.amazon.com/gp/product/0978533933/ref=dbs_a_def_rwt_bibl_vppi_i0

"I am not even completely through this book but it is a page turner for sure. I am about 3/4 of the way through it. I am a mother and was intrigued to read this as I've felt from a very young age that mothers were given intuition by God to lead, guide, and care for their young. What has me floored is how much scripture actually does point to this beautiful truth that I've known to be true. The author has done a wonderful job of bringing these verses to light!"

"Samuel Martin's first Thy Rod and thy Staff book was the first gentle parenting book I read and it was like a breath of fresh air. I've always felt like there was something wrong with so many Christians using scriptures to say that the Bible tells us to spank. When I came across that book everything made so much sense. Samuel Martin is very thorough and explains things from a biblical perspective in great detail. This book has been a huge blessing as well and it has made me feel more confident in following those God given instincts as a wife and mother. May God bless the Author and may God bless others with the teachings in this book!"

"Beautifully written, enlightening content"

About the Author

Samuel Martin was born in England and is the youngest child of Dr. Ernest L. and Helen R. Martin, who are both Americans and natives of the state of Oklahoma.

He lived in the UK for the first seven years of his life before moving to the USA with his family. He lived in the USA until 2001 when he married a native Israeli Christian and relocated to live in Jerusalem, where he currently resides.

He and his wife, Sonia, have two daughters.

His experience with biblical scholarship began at an early age. His father lead a program in conjunction with Hebrew University and the late Professor Benjamin Mazar, where over a five year period, some 450 college students came to work on an archaeological excavation in Jerusalem starting in 1969.

Since that first trip, Samuel has visited Israel on 14 different occasions living more than 19 years of his life in the country. He has toured all areas of Israel as well as worked in several archaeological excavations.

He writes regularly on biblical subjects with a particular interest in children, families, nature, science, the Bible, and gender in the Biblical context. He holds an MA from the University of the Holy Land in Inter-Cultural Studies and the Bible.

Website: www.biblechild.com
Contact: info@biblechild.com
Facebook: https://www.facebook.com/byblechyld/
Blog: www.samuelmartin.blogspot.com
Amazon: https://www.amazon.com/Samuel-Martin/e/B00HP94ZZA/ref=dp_byline_cont_book_1